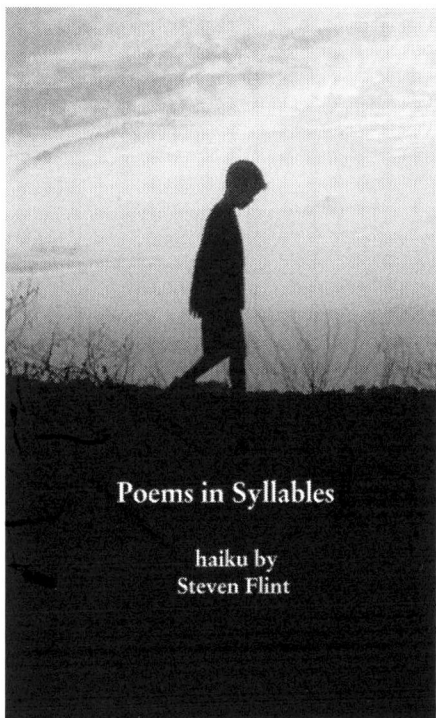

Poems in Syllables

haiku by
Steven Flint

For Sigalit

Steven Flint, author of
The Sun and the Boy
Lev Loveheart
and twelve collections of haiku poetry

Poems in Syllables

I want to travel
in your story, I want to
rest between your words

The mystery of
love brought us together, like
clues to a riddle

Within my own mind,
the circles I have travelled
all lead back to you

My favourite word,
I pronounce your name slowly,
absorbed by its sound

Poems about love,
I saw them all in your eyes
like a flash of light

On rare occasions,
the universe contracts to
a single heartbeat

All we have are words,
they're written in our eyes or
spoken in silence

I know I don't know,
the only thing I'm sure of
is uncertainty

Let go of the past,
it's time for the ghost to rest,
your life is calling

The sun blew a kiss,
my heart skipped a beat as I
remembered summer

I saw the moon rise
from the corner of your smile
and eclipse my heart

Dreams slowly ripen
in the orchard of your eyes,
like a wish come true

You wrote a poem
on the petal of a rose
that bloomed in my heart

I caught the autumn
leaf that fell from your smile, I
keep it just for luck

Dream of a life when
the world is a place where we
can live in a dream

I read my fortune
in the palm of your hand, it
said our stars align

Diving into the
magic of your aqua soul,
soothed by your ocean

The fire in your eyes
melted all my resistance
to your inner charm

A consummate love,
where I dissolve in you and
you dissolve in me

I listened to the
poems of nature read by
the sun in the sky

This strawberry heart,
it's ripe with the sweetness of
love, come take a bite

Orchestral music,
a sweet articulation
of life's sublime force

Wisdom is Knowing
Humanity is Being
Living is Doing

Write me a poem,
bottle the essence of love
in ink on paper

Converging ripples,
incidental physics linked
our expanding hearts

Metamorphosis,
from lava to butterflies,
strangers to lovers

Spare me doom and gloom,
give me knuckle hard poems
that will change the world

Imagination,
it is the greatest playground
your mind will enter

It's like autumn fire,
her auburn hair burns mood red,
a warm carmine blaze

Winter sky ice blue,
the fields are covered in snow
naked trees play dead

In love's firmament,
where you end and I begin
margins can't be found

The language of touch
the healing contact of souls,
wonderful closeness

Eggshell lives we have,
as delicate as snowflakes
one puff and we're gone

When we sit and talk
an old book of magic spells
opens in your eyes

Yesterday has gone
Tomorrow is just a dream
only Now has truth

I dare you to come
on a journey without maps,
we'll follow the stars

Moment by moment,
it's all just an illusion
time stands still, minds move

The flower in my
garden was planted by you,
a poem that bloomed

Send me a postcard
from paradise, let me know
you arrived safely

Aloft in darkness,
a calm moon softens the night
with its white silence

The creak of floorboards,
a draft under the door, this
house whispers at night

The moon writes love songs,
serenades for starlight with
you at the chorus

The book in my heart
is full of scarlet poems
all written for you

My winter snowflake,
gentle and pure, she has a
beauty of her own

I saw the ripples
blow over the surface of
your mind like silk wind

Through the midnight rain
I see a warm light in the
window of your soul

I hear your thoughts, like
a subtext to our silence,
words below whispers

The rising moon comes
like the first dream of the night
spreading white magic

I spoke your name and
you heard a voice in the wind,
an echo from home

The moss on the stone
has grown thick since you left, time
is at a standstill

I saw you dreaming,
I watched your eyes smolder in
quiet reverie

No ocean is as
deep as your love, no gold is
as pure as your heart

Your home is the wind,
open a door and let your
worries blow away

Feel without touching,
speak without saying a word,
know without looking

The love in your heart,
like a drop of water that
contains an ocean

A man was drowning
in your eyes, I looked closer
and saw it was me

The nomad in my
heart wants to wander through the
landscape of your soul

A north wind brought you
to my door, a summer breeze
carried you away

How many lifetimes
before this one did I first
fall in love with you ?

You didn't warn me
of the whirlpool in your eyes,
you just let me swim

Sometimes the only
way to hold on to someone
is to let them go

A dream, although just
a dream, still has its moment
in reality

Your body is a
musical instrument, stop
and listen within

The constellation
of youth still shines bright in the
window of her eyes

You must follow your
dream, it's the most likely path
to your happiness

You are the poem
I dreamed I could write, but still
you elude my words

As you leave, something
catches my eye, then I see
you're taking my dreams

Excavate my heart
and you will find the remains
of a long lost love

I was the schoolboy
daydreaming at the window
waiting for the bell

Michelangelo,
he saw you buried in stone
freed you with his art

Just after midnight,
in the stillness of the hour
I hear you dreaming

The sound of the wind,
the quiet before the storm,
the charge of the rain

Leave a flower in
the barrel of a gun, tell
them war is over

Born for greater things,
like a butterfly punching
through chrysalis walls

A cloud in the sky,
a wave on the sea, and you
a leaf on the breeze

From the vineyard in
my heart, we can harvest the
Cabernet of love

My ears absorb the
transcontinental whisper
of a foreign breeze

I was falling through
your moonlight, catching the stars
tangled in your smile

Love is so vibrant,
it's the poet's mission to
craft words with heartbeats

You're the thief of hearts,
I dreamed that you stole mine, it
was the perfect crime

Time became a snail,
rust grew thick around the hours,
days took weeks to pass

Marooned in a dream,
me on your desert island
waving ships goodbye

Autumn's blue again,
the leaves have ended their love
affair with the trees

I was the salt, you
were the water, we were the
sea, one endless wave

Don't judge me by the
things I did wrong, judge me by
the things I made right

Our star burnt out long
ago, but its light still shines
in my heart today

I have always been
a dreamer, sometimes asleep
I feel wide awake

A blue pearl held in
the palm of the universe,
our precious home, Earth

You are the autumn
poem I could never write,
my tree without leaves

Love letters composed
in your tantric handwriting
consumed fire with fire

For this I was born,
to be a recipient
of your endless Love

Cinematic shows,
I watched the film in your eyes,
your star performance

The clues from heaven,
starlight perforates darkness
angels point upwards

I can't define you,
as I can't describe the way
you perfect my life

Love is a vast sea,
I throw my bottled message
and wait for replies

This poem is yours,
it belonged to you before
I ever wrote it

You keep it well hid,
but I can see crumbs of love
sprinkled on your lips

No one else will do,
there's a compass in my heart
it points towards you

An expectant moon,
her belly swells with each night
she gives birth to stars

We all merit Love,
it is the substance from which
we were created

Looking back, its hard
to discern between a dream
and a memory

Born in crimson peace,
we all have a poppy heart
in which to find rest

Such sweet turbulence,
the hearts wild cacophony
of orchestral love

Fools roam aimlessly
hoping coincidence will
be kind to their lives

We can do little,
but a little is better
than nothing at all

That spark in your eyes
could ignite a deep love in
my tinder box heart

Perplexed by darkness,
you made a compass from stars
and found the way home

I add you to the
vocabulary of my
moonlight poetry

Like Chinese lanterns,
I saw the light in your eyes
from lifetimes away

I grow through the cracks
of my fears and faults, like a
resilient flower

Sitting on the fence,
still undecided which grass
is looking greener

I collect words like
others collect butterflies,
I prize their beauty

Look up at the sky,
I gave you half of the moon,
you kept every star

Prologue to a life
Dialogues on how to live
Epilogue of why

A broken heart is
such a silent disaster,
few ever suspect

Did you ever feel
a complete symphony in
a single heartbeat ?

I can look into
the mystery of your eyes
and see lives gone by

What's at the end of
the universe ? Perhaps love,
what else could there be ?

You are heaven scent
named after sacred flowers
Jasmine Lilac Rose

The curve of your neck
the bend of your smile, the curl
in your hair, round joys

Personality
Individuality
Authenticity

Teardrop love stories,
Romeo and Juliet
have nothing on us

I discovered a
parallel universe in
the stars of your eyes

I count the seasons
blowing through your eyes, winter
spring, summer and fall

Ice may slowly melt,
the wind can blow hot or cold,
but you remain true

You are the lighthouse
guiding me safely through life's
tempestuous sea

I look into the
silence of your eyes and trip
through the universe

I rearranged the
words in the dictionary
to make a novel

You left a footprint
in the sand of my heart that
no time can erase

If you break my heart
do it the old fashioned way,
gentle with the pain

The swans in my heart
dream of the calm blue lake that
resides in your eyes

Listen what happens
when nothing happens at all,
things fall into place

There's no need to knock,
my heart is an open door
it was never locked

Your hands are like doves
flying through my soul, they calm
my fears and bring peace

I was once a bird
flying in search of freedom,
now I am the sky

I lost you once and
found you again in the taut
strings of my guitar

Love arithmetic,
an intimate equation
where $2 = 1$

Indigo secrets
whispered to a poet's heart
inspire velvet dreams

Your eyes reveal a
silent soliloquy in
a play with my heart

Your beauty allures
me like the intricacy
of a summer rose

Life, just when you think
you have it under your thumb
it throws a curve ball

This song is for you,
gentle soul left behind in
the leaves of autumn

My minds playing tricks,
are you the real deal or
just an illusion ?

One day, we will all
live on in the memory
of the computer

You're touching my life
with your soul from far away
and still it moves me

That first attraction,
you try not to look too much,
but you are staring

Among the bones of
old beliefs and long lost dreams,
a phoenix takes flight

Daydreams about you
they keep me awake at night,
my muse outshines sleep

I thought it was luck,
but this strange coincidence
could only be fate

The lessons I learned
were the chronicles of love
dictated by you

Darkness is fractured
by soft blows of morning light,
sunrise breaks silence

Graphite confessions,
penciled musings of my thoughts,
cursive disclosures

A thing of beauty,
like a misplaced angel that
lightens the darkness

The shipping forecast,
Fair Isle, variable 6,
occasional gale

Your footsteps clicking
down the pavement of my life,
now that's a heartbeat

That faraway look,
a migrating bird leaving
the nest of your eyes

I followed a light
into the brown mist of your
eyes and touched your soul

She asked a question,
How much do you value love ?
With my life, I said

For a night or two
we can sit by the firelight
and watch stars ignite

Times change forever,
these hands won't always reach you
my heart surely will

The heart finds itself
in the heart of another
uncovered by love

Sunset afterglow,
you're the echo of a dream
still ringing in time

That was my mistake,
I waited for you to ask,
but you never did

I feel your presence
as if you are beside me,
a warm spectral love

In our lifetime we
turned pages of history
and left a footnote

The scent of heaven,
I heard flowers in your voice
the flora of sound

Given enough time,
the softness of the water
shapes the hardest stone

These odd chance meetings,
strange twists of coincidence
life's sweet happenstance

In a sapphire dream
a blue moon rose in her eyes
and conquered my sky

Autumn afternoon,
the wind clips a leaf with the
soft parting of time

If I can trust, I
can believe, if I believe
then I can succeed

She's classic autumn,
as auburn as October
in amber sunlight

Come back yesterday,
I'll give you tomorrow if
you return today

I know I am home,
the reflection in your eyes
is so familiar

Be a passenger
in the taxi of my heart,
I'll drive you back home

Choose your poison and
writhe in ecstasy, one life
baby, make it count

Bathe us in your Light
soften our hearts with your Love
reward us with Life

We are the conduits
of celestial light, our hearts
shine like temple lamps

If I should sleepwalk
into your dream, don't wake up
before morning calls

The light from your smile
was one of your best poems,
I knew you could write

That calm melody,
I love the sound of the sea,
liquid symphonies

The light around my
light comes from her, she makes a
home for my shadow

When I can't find you
I will look for you in the
poems you leave me

You're making a sound
in my heart, but you can't hear
the music I feel

Nothing is by chance,
subconscious maneuvering
brought us together

I dreamed about you,
sleep brought you back to me like
a gift from the night

The credence of love,
I can see it in your eyes
calm, still, unerring

Just after midnight,
in the stillness of the hour
I hear you dreaming

cover photo by Gila Koller

Made in the USA
Las Vegas, NV
11 December 2021